FAST FACT MATH

FAST FACT SUBTRACTION

8 TOTAL JELLY BEANS
MINUS 5 JELLY BEANS

8 − 5 =
3 JELLY BEANS
LEFT

BY BLANCHE ROESSER

Gareth Stevens
PUBLISHING

Please visit our website, www.garethstevens.com. For a free color catalog of all our high-quality books, call toll free 1-800-542-2595 or fax 1-877-542-2596.

Library of Congress Cataloging-in-Publication Data

Names: Roesser, Blanche, author.
Title: Fast fact subtraction / Blanche Roesser.
Description: New York : Gareth Stevens Publishing, [2019] | Series: Fast fact math |
Includes index.
Identifiers: LCCN 2017040798| ISBN 9781538219911 (library bound) | ISBN
9781538219935 (pbk.) | ISBN 9781538219942 (6 pack)
Subjects: LCSH: Subtraction–Juvenile literature. | Arithmetic–Juvenile literature.
Classification: LCC QA115 .R6728 2019 | DDC 513.2/12–dc23 LC record available at https://lccn.loc.
gov/2017040798First Edition

Published in 2019 by
Gareth Stevens Publishing
111 East 14th Street, Suite 349
New York, NY 10003

Designer: Sarah Liddell
Editor: Therese Shea

Photo credits: Cover, p. 1 mayakova/Shutterstock.com; chalkboard texture used throughout mexrix/
Shutterstock.com; p. 5 Jason Stitt/Shutterstock.com; p. 9 Dmussman/Shutterstock.com; p. 11 (both)
Monkey Business Images/Shuttestock.com; p. 17 vectorfusionart/Shutterstock.com; p. 19 sonya
etchison/Shutterstock.com; p. 21 VGstockstudio/Shutterstock.com.

Printed in the United States of America

CPSIA compliance information: Batch #CS18GS: For further information contact Gareth Stevens, New York, New York at 1-800-542-2595.

CONTENTS

Words in the glossary appear in **bold** type the first time they are used in the text.

TAKE IT AWAY

Subtraction is a part of life. You probably don't even think about using this math **operation**, but you use it all the time. Imagine you have a handful of jelly beans. Each time you pop one into your mouth, you're subtracting 1 from the whole amount.

Math becomes easier to understand when you understand how you can use it—or are using it—every day. This book will teach you several "fast facts" of subtraction and show you how to become an **expert** subtracter!

MATH MANIA!

As you read this book, you'll be the master subtracter. Get ready to use your subtraction skills. Look for the upside-down answers to check your work. Good luck!

IF YOU POP TWO JELLY BEANS INTO YOUR MOUTH AT A TIME, YOU'RE SUBTRACTING BY 2.

SUBTRACTION WORDS

FAST FACT: When you subtract one number from another, the number that you get is called the difference.

FAST FACT: The minuend is the number that is subtracted from. The subtrahend is the number that is subtracted.

FAST FACT: Subtraction problems can be written different ways.

Sometimes, subtraction **equations** are written vertically, or up and down:

$$\begin{array}{r} 23 \\ -\ 3 \\ \hline 20 \end{array}$$

Sometimes, they're written horizontally, or in a line:

$$23 - 3 = 20$$

No matter how it's written, the answer—or the difference—is the same.

THESE ARE THE SPECIAL NAMES FOR THE NUMBERS IN A SUBTRACTION EQUATION.

SUBTRAHEND

$$5 - 2 = 3$$

MINUEND

DIFFERENCE

MATH MANIA!

In the subtraction equation below, which number is the minuend? Which is the subtrahend? Which is the difference?

$$
\begin{array}{r}
982 \\
- 82 \\
\hline
900
\end{array}
$$

Answer: 982 is the minuend, 82 is the subtrahend, 900 is the difference

OPPOSITES

Let's see why. Start with the addition sentence below:

$$52 + 2 = 54$$

If you take away 2 from the sum, you undo the addition:

$$54 - 2 = 52$$

You end up with 52, the number you started with in the addition equation.

The math word for "opposite" is "inverse." So, you can say that subtraction is the inverse operation of addition. That just means subtraction **reverses** the effect of addition.

8

MATH MANIA!

"Undo" the addition equations to complete the subtraction equations below.

$$77 + 11 = 88$$
$$88 - 11 = \ ?$$

$$10 + 63 = 73$$
$$73 - 63 = \ ?$$

Answer: 88 − 11 = 77, 73 − 63 = 10

THERE ARE MANY OPPOSITES IN YOUR WORLD. FAST AND SLOW AND BIG AND SMALL ARE JUST TWO EXAMPLES. CAN YOU THINK OF MORE?

FACT FAMILIES

Sometimes, fact families are called number families. For each group of three numbers, you can create two addition and two subtraction number facts. Look at the fact family below:

$$17 + 3 = 20$$
$$3 + 17 = 20$$
$$20 - 17 = 3$$
$$20 - 3 = 17$$

Fact families are another way to see how addition and subtraction are **related**.

MATH MANIA!

$$33 + 9 = 42$$
$$9 + 33 = 42$$
$$42 - 9 = 33$$

Which fact is missing from the fact family above?

a. $42 - 33 = 9$
b. $42 + 9 = 51$
c. $33 + 42 = 75$
d. $33 - 9 = 24$

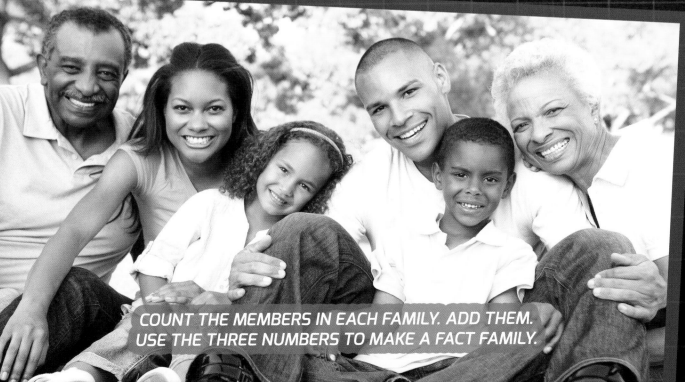

COUNT THE MEMBERS IN EACH FAMILY. ADD THEM. USE THE THREE NUMBERS TO MAKE A FACT FAMILY.

CHECK IT OUT

Let's start with a subtraction equation:

$$
\begin{array}{r}
37 \\
- 12 \\
\hline
25
\end{array}
$$

To check your work, start with the difference, 25. Then, add the number you subtracted. If the sum equals the number you subtracted from, you're correct:

$$
\begin{array}{r}
25 \\
+ 12 \\
\hline
37
\end{array}
$$

Try again with larger numbers:

$$
\begin{array}{r}
647 \\
- 236 \\
\hline
411
\end{array}
\qquad
\begin{array}{r}
411 \\
+ 236 \\
\hline
647
\end{array}
$$

It worked again! Use this method to check your work.

YOU CAN ALSO USE SUBTRACTION TO CHECK YOUR ADDITION! START WITH
THE SUM AND SUBTRACT ONE OF THE NUMBERS THAT WERE ADDED TOGETHER.
IT SHOULD EQUAL THE OTHER NUMBER IN THE ADDITION PROBLEM.

$$
\begin{array}{r}
345 \\
+\ 612 \\
\hline
957
\end{array}
\qquad
\begin{array}{r}
957 \\
-\ 612 \\
\hline
345
\end{array}
$$

MATH MANIA! ◄//

Solve the subtraction problem below. Then, create and solve
an addition equation to check your work.

$$
\begin{array}{r}
476 \\
-\ 365 \\
\hline
?
\end{array}
$$

Answer: 111, 111 + 365 = 476

13

CHANGE IT!

Subtraction can be tricky when a **column** of numbers has a smaller number on top. In this problem, 4 is smaller than 9:

$$\begin{array}{r} 24 \\ -\ 9 \\ \hline ? \end{array}$$

There are several ways to solve this. One way is to add the same amount to each number. In this case, add 1 to 24 and 1 to 9:

$$\begin{array}{r} 25 \\ -10 \\ \hline ? \end{array}$$

It's much easier to solve this. The answer is 15.

14

YOU CAN SEE WHY 24 – 9 IS THE SAME PROBLEM AS 25 – 10 WHEN YOU LOOK AT A NUMBER LINE. YOU'RE SHIFTING THE NUMBERS IN YOUR PROBLEM BY 1. HOWEVER, THE SAME AMOUNT OF NUMBERS REMAINS BETWEEN THE NUMBERS IN YOUR NEW PROBLEM.

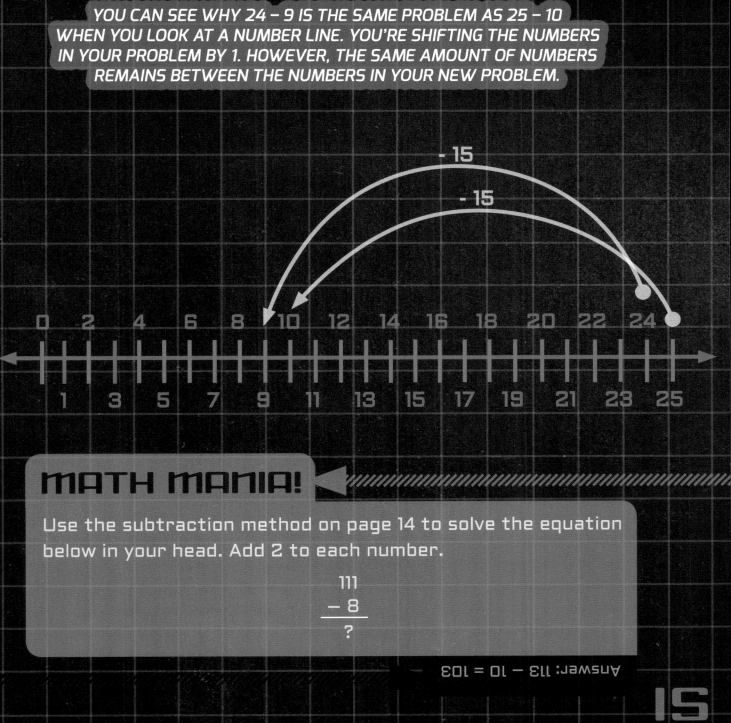

- 15

- 15

0 2 4 6 8 10 12 14 16 18 20 22 24
1 3 5 7 9 11 13 15 17 19 21 23 25

MATH MANIA!

Use the subtraction method on page 14 to solve the equation below in your head. Add 2 to each number.

$$\begin{array}{r} 111 \\ -\ 8 \\ \hline ? \end{array}$$

IT'S THE IDENTITY

This fast fact is called the identity property of subtraction. An identity is a number that when added, subtracted, multiplied, or divided with any number allows the number to remain the same. In subtraction, the identity is 0.

Let's see how this property, or rule, works in some subtraction equations:

$$32 - 0 = 32 \qquad 118 - 0 = 118$$
$$85 - 0 = 85 \qquad 999 - 0 = 999$$

Think of the largest number you can. Now subtract 0. Did the number get any smaller? No!

MATH MANIA!

Use the identity property of subtraction to complete the subtraction equations below.

$$191 - 0 = ?$$
$$89 - ? = 89$$
$$? - 0 = 44$$

HAVE YOU HEARD OF A SECRET IDENTITY? IDENTITIES IN MATH AREN'T A SECRET! IN BOTH ADDITION AND SUBTRACTION, THE IDENTITY IS 0.

SUBTRACTING PROBLEMS

FAST FACT: Subtraction word problems use different words and phrases to tell you to subtract.

Some of these subtraction words are:

take away	left
difference	fewer than
minus	remain
less than	how many more

Read this subtraction word problem:

There were 87 geese flying south for the winter. Then, 32 of the geese flew away. How many geese were left?

The word "left" tells us to set up a subtraction problem:

$$87 - 32 = ?$$

The difference is 55, so 55 geese were left.

MATH MANIA!

Solve the word problem below.
(Hint: This is a two-step problem.)

The school bus had 37 children on it. The bus stopped and 12 children got off. It stopped again and 5 more children got off. How many children remained on the school bus?

$$37 - 12 = x$$
$$x - 5 = ?$$

MASTER SUBTRACTER!

People who work in stores use subtraction all the [tim]e. For example, **cashiers** may have to make change [wh]en a **customer** gives them too much money for a [pro]duct. They may have to figure out how many products [are] left in the store, too. In fact, almost every job requires [so]me subtraction.

If you keep using subtraction every day, you'll be [rea]dy to take on any problem—and any future job. You'll [be] a master subtracter!

MATH MANIA!

Solve this two-step subtraction word problem.

Anthony had $20. He bought a game. He received $10 back. He bought another game, gave $10 to the cashier, and received $3 back. How much did the first game cost? How much did the second game cost?

first game = n
second game = t

$20 − n = $10 $10 − t = $3

IT'S GOOD TO KNOW HOW MUCH MONEY YOU SHOULD BE GETTING BACK AT A STORE. SUBTRACTION CAN HELP!

GLOSSARY

cashier: someone who works in a store and handles customers' money

column: a group of things written one under another down a page

customer: someone who buys goods or services from a business

equation: a statement in math that two values are equal

expert: a person who has a special skill or knowledge about a subject

operation: a mathematical process (such as addition or multiplication) that is used for getting one number or set of numbers from others according to a rule

related: connected in some way

reverse: to change something to an opposite state

solve: to find the correct answer for

FOR MORE INFORMATION

BOOKS

Becker, Ann. *Subtraction.* New York, NY: Crabtree Publishing, 2010.

Marzollo, Jean. *Help Me Learn Subtraction.* New York, NY: Holiday House, 2012.

Penn, M. W. *It's Subtraction!* Mankato, MN: Capstone Press, 2012.

WEBSITES

Math Games: Subtraction
www.mathgames.com/subtraction
Find several grade levels of subtraction games here.

Subtract Numbers Up to Three Digits
www.ixl.com/math/grade-3/subtract-numbers-up-to-three-digits
Race the clock while answering these subtraction problems.

INDEX